Praise for
Workbook for a Career in Wildlife and Natural Resource Conservation

"After reading and thoroughly enjoying this book by my good friend and trusted colleague Carrol Henderson, I wholeheartedly recommend this companion booklet to students considering a career in wildlife conservation, be it as a manager, researcher or educator! It should serve as an important tool in helping you succeed and as a must have to those coming into the profession but also by university faculty for guiding career plans, strategies and goals. I plan to begin using it in my college wildlife classroom immediately after publication!"

-Dr. Bill Faber, professor of wildlife, Brainerd Vocational Tech, Brainerd, MN

Carrol Henderson's new book is an invaluable resource for anyone passionate about managing and restoring wildlife and biodiversity. The book weaves the themes of love, teach, learn and integrity into a comprehensive guide for a successful career in natural resource conservation. Through Carrol's heartfelt anecdotes and practical advice, it encourages readers to follow their hearts and pursue conservation because "it is the right thing to do!".

Carrol's love for wildlife inspires readers to cultivate their own passion for nature. The emphasis on teaching and learning underscores the importance of continuous education and mentorship in this field. With guidance on navigating the various facets of a career in conservation, this book serves as a beacon for current and aspiring conservationists, offering insights and inspiration on everything from fieldwork and research to advocacy and policymaking.

In the face of ongoing environmental issues, Carrol reminds us that "attitude is everything" when addressing ecological challenges and the role each of us can play in creating sustainable solutions. This book is more than just a career manual; it is a call to action for those dedicated to preserving our precious ecosystems. It stands as a testament to the power of doing what is right, guided by love and a commitment to lifelong learning. This book is an essential read for anyone committed to making a difference in the world of wildlife conservation.

-Dr. Alexis Grinde, PhD, research program manager and wildlife ecologist, Natural Resources Research Institute (NRRI), Duluth, Minnesota

I find no fault whatsoever in your twenty life lessons – indeed, my own version would parallel yours almost exactly! Your emphasis on following your heart, keeping your antennae out for new opportunities and connections, recognizing serendipity and capturing it, focusing on big themes and goals, not micromanaging and always be reading – these are profound life values that apply well beyond the science, wildlife and conservation fields that have defined your life and mine. As the great architect and city planner Daniel Burnham famously wrote, "Make no little plans. They have no magic to stir men's blood and probably will not themselves be realized. Make big plans, aim high in hope and work…" I have long adhered to this philosophy about life, work and aspirations. It is clear that you have as well, Carrol, and your results over the decades attest to the success of your approach. Congratulations on sharing both with the world in the form of these lessons.

–Dr. John W. Fitzpatrick, Professor, Ecology and Evolutionary Biology, Cornell University; Emeritus Director, Cornell Lab of Ornithology, Ithaca, New York

Across every page of his writings, his exuberance for life and the opportunities to make a difference each day ushers in is refreshing and a welcome salve for readers from all walks of life, eager for optimism and real-world examples and tools for how to find and use your voice for nature and a better world.

As America's 90+ million birders and anyone who loves and appreciates nature and its wild wonders look to one another and to our neighbors for inspiration as we endeavor to recover the three billion birds that have been lost since 1970, Carrol

Henderson offers an inspirational, practical rubric as we follow a guided tour, from the conservation legend himself, giving us the gift of his *Why* and *How*; pulling back the curtains, and inspiring us with a cadre of lessons hard earned and learned through the course of a remarkable career. Carrol has certainly fulfilled his obligation of leaving things better than what he found it, and then some.

–Marshall Johnson, Chief Conservation Officer, National Audubon Society; Science, Policy, Conservation and Chapter engagement.

Regardless of whether you are a student interested in a career in Natural Resources, an advisor of such students, or someone looking for thoughtful advice on living a successful life; Carrol's advice will serve you well. Drawn from a lifetime of service to our natural resources, Carrol uses these experiences to highlight the approaches that allowed him to help shape how Minnesota managed its public trust resources so successfully. Rarely does one person leave such an expansive professional footprint, yet with this book Carrol will further add to that legacy and continue to help future generations carry on his work.

–Dr. Brian J. Hiller, Professor of Biology, Wildlife Specialist

WORKBOOK
for a Career in Wildlife and Natural Resource Conservation

Wisdom
Editions
Minneapolis

WORKBOOK
for a Career in Wildlife and Natural Resource Conservation

Carrol L. Henderson

Wisdom
Editions
Minneapolis

Table of Contents

Foreword   1

Introduction   5

Life Lesson 1   9
Follow your passion, study what you love and love what you do. That is where you will find success.

Life Lesson 2   19
Choosing a grad school. If you want to be the best, learn from the best: "Learn from the one who wrote the book!"

Life Lesson 3   25
Cross-pollinate your grad school major

Life Lesson 4   29
Develop personal skill sets that will enhance your career

Life Lesson 5   41
Find the mentors in your midst who will share their vision, perspective and lifelong passion for nature

Life Lesson 6   49
In picking your job, don't follow the dollars. Follow your heart

Life Lesson 7   55
Learn to *Connect the Dots!* Learn to connect two apparently unrelated facts or ideas to solve a problem

Life Lesson 8   63
Know your publics

Life Lesson 9   69
Keep a healthy balance between your professional and personal life

Life Lesson 10   75
Channel your energies, keep the big picture in mind, think big and be patient

Life Lesson 11   81
A problem is just an opportunity that needs to be repackaged. *Attitude is everything!*

Life Lesson 12   89
Keep a Four-H strategy to balance your conservation program

Life Lesson 13   93
Stealth Mode

Life Lesson 14   97
Use the *Multiplier Effect* to spread your conservation messages

Life Lesson 15   101
Your success is determined by the extent to which your employees are successful in fulfilling their goals

Life Lesson 16   109
Always have a *pet project*

Life Lesson 17   113
Most important wildlife conservation and restoration efforts require not just years, but decades, to accomplish

Life Lesson 18   119
Read voraciously. *(A room without books is like a body without a soul. –Marcus Tullius Cicero)*.

Life Lesson 19   123
Some of life's greatest opportunities and revelations come wrapped in a blanket of pure serendipity

Life Lesson 20   131
Become acquainted with existing laws protecting wildlife and endangered species so you can assist with court proceedings and development of legislation

About the Author   135

Foreword

Marshall Johnson,
Chief Conservation Officer, National Audubon Society,
Science, Policy, Conservation and Chapter Engagement

I have been blessed to work alongside many amazing conservation, community and business leaders, ever since one faithful morning where I found myself enthralled by the booming, dancing mating ritual of the greater prairie chicken: my spark bird.

Upon arriving in Minnesota as a teenager, I quickly noted two endearing traits seemingly inherent to the state: The goodness of the people, and their passion for wildlife and the outdoors. Minnesota is a state defined by its natural beauty and iconic species such as the common loon, northern cardinal and trumpeter swan, to name but a few. Equally so, the people of the state embody a sense of care, innovation, excellence, diversity and a desire to generally leave something better than one found it. These are almost a prerequisite for citizenship. Perhaps no leader embodies these traits as profoundly as Carrol Henderson.

One struggles to adequately describe the enormity of Carrol Henderson's contributions to wildlife conservation, wildlife awareness, and species recovery; and while Minnesota has been the canvas upon which Carrol's art of action has come to life, the impacts of his contributions have and will continue to be felt across the hemisphere.

His work is felt by North St. Louis County teenagers in Missouri who flock to the confluence of the Missouri and Mississippi Rivers each winter to glimpse thousands of trumpeter swans, riverine dignitaries, many of who make their way from the lakes of Minnesota, where their existence was once on the brink of extirpation.

Perhaps you are one of the many thousands more female biologists across state wildlife agencies who have been inspired by the example set by the extraordinary team of women hired by Carrol at a time when this was anything but the norm. It's hard to truly gauge the far-reaching impact of Carrol's leadership in this regard.

Given the significant role of Minnesota's state nongame program in the Department of Natural Resources, perhaps you are coming to this reading as someone who dutifully checks the box on your tax returns, opting to do your part for the state's nongame wildlife – if not, you should!

Dedicating one's life to the preservation of wildlife and wild places can be painstaking, grueling work, but for nearly fifty years Carrol has stood as the personification of a happy warrior, innovating, advocating and building relationships on behalf of nature and her special critters.

As you begin your journey with Carrol, I leave you with the wisdom of the Lorax: *Unless someone like you cares a whole awful lot, Nothing is going to get better. It's not.* Carrol Henderson sure cared for nature and her song, a whole awful lot.

Introduction

Looking back on my forty-four-year wildlife conservation career in the Minnesota Department of Natural Resources (DNR) and another six years of conservation activism since retirement, I wish to share fifty years of strategies I incorporated into my priorities, goals and conservation projects. I synthesized those experiences into twenty *life lessons* that have contributed to successful conservation efforts. These lessons began evolving in 2003 when I started making annual presentations for the Honors Mentor Connection class of the Gifted Education Services Program in Plymouth, Minnesota. The program was managed by Dr. Dorothy Welch. She invited me every year to give a presentation to talented and gifted high school seniors from thirteen Intermediate District 287 high schools in the southern and southwestern regions of the Twin

Cities. Each year through 2018 I gave a one-hour oral presentation to over twenty-five seniors that resulted into the following *Life Lessons*. They could be helpful for aspiring high school and college students hungry for tips on preparing for their careers. It may include natural resource students, as well as beginning wildlife managers, biologists and conservationists as they proceed with their careers. The life lessons could also be helpful for many other careers not related to natural resource conservation. Dr. Welch deserves credit for encouraging me to summarize how I have approached my career and conservation projects in these Life Lessons. My goal in sharing these experiences was not so much to relate *what* I have done over the course of my career but to share my insights on *how* these projects were accomplished by applying those life lessons.

Carrol Henderson and a trumpeter swan ready for release in Minnesota

Life Lesson 1
Follow your passion, study what you love and love what you do. That is where you will find success.

Picking a university and your major

When entering Iowa State, I selected engineering science because friends discouraged me from studying natural resources and wildlife conservation because they said those careers offered low pay and few jobs. Bad choice. Bad advice. I signed up for a major in engineering science, but I felt low motivation. After one quarter, I changed my major to zoology with minors in botany and physics. There was a dramatic change in my perspective! After changing majors, my grade point and attitude improved dramatically.

My son Craig also provided a lesson in selecting what university to attend.

Craig Henderson enjoying nature in Costa Rica. He is also a graduate of MIT.

Our son Craig enrolled in the University of Minnesota Talented Youth Mathematics Program in middle school. By the time he graduated from high school he had earned thirty college credits including calculus from the University of Minnesota. He also took a special math course in high school summer school at Michigan Tech. His professor there asked him about his choice for college. Craig said he was considering Iowa State, Harvey Mudd and Caltech, but he seemed uncertain with his response. His professor asked where he would really like to go. Craig said he would really like to go to MIT, but he didn't know if he was good enough to go to MIT. His professor responded, "If you are not good enough to go to MIT, make them tell you that you are not good enough! Why settle for silver when you can go for the gold!"

Craig scored well in his college entrance tests in math. He applied to MIT and got accepted! He earned a B.S. and MEng from MIT. He has worked for several major corporations providing IT expertise. Don't sell yourself short in considering your academic career. Look for the best faculty and academic program that matches your career aspirations. *Go for the gold!* Within the scope of your *dream* or *reach schools*, it is also a good strategy to apply to a balanced spectrum of *safety* and *target* schools that can help you achieve your career goals.

Mentorship presentation responses

"Don't settle for silver if you can go for the gold." This quote by Mr. Henderson has inspired me to try the best I can do in everything that I do.

I agree with you when you said that it's important to pick a career that fits your interest because it should drive you to do amazing things...Another thing I took away from your presentation was to learn, love and teach what you do. In other words, create something amazing and share it with the world.

Many people have said to "follow your heart," but I haven't heard anyone share their experiences, successes and passion when following their dreams the way Carrol Henderson did. When you see just how happy someone else is doing something they love, it sticks with you a lot more.

Mr. Henderson made it clear to me that I should choose a career field that I feel deeply passionate about, because I am going to have to love it and do it for the rest of my working life! Another part in Mr. Henderson's speech made me question everything that I have been telling myself when he said "Why settle for silver, when you can go for the gold?" This whole year I have been debating on whether or not to apply to certain universities because I just figured they wouldn't accept me because I didn't get a twenty-eight or higher on my ACT or have a 4.0 GPA. But when he told us that why settle for something less, when you could have much more, I almost felt guilty for telling myself this whole year that I shouldn't apply to those challenging universities because basically I wasn't good enough in my mind, and that I was just supposed to face this reality that those universities truly only care about exceptional grades. Hearing about Mr. Henderson's career, which is something he actually does love, made me have some hope that there is a career out there for me where I can maybe come close to accomplishing the things he has in his career, while loving my career at the same time.

I was intrigued by the stories from your childhood and how a childhood hobby turned into your life passion. You are a pioneer for conservation in the state of Minnesota and, for that, Minnesota will always be thankful for your hard work and dedication.

Workbook questions and notes

1. It is desirable to begin this quest in your junior year in high school to get the information you need for making a decision on your college or university of choice.

2. List the animals or habitats that are of particular interest to you.

_____

_____

_____

_____

_____

3. Are there any jobs or professions you are interested in pursuing relative to the outdoors and nature?

4. Are there any local conservationists who could be consulted about their career choice?

5. Are there any local natural resources offices or county, state or federal natural resource offices where biologists could be consulted about careers?

6. As you consider your options for higher education and a lifetime career, you face many alternatives, including lots of suggestions from family and friends. As

you evaluate the benefits and disadvantages
of each major decision like what college
or university you should attend, consider
making a spreadsheet to compare the
benefits and disadvantages of each school.

_____

_____

_____

_____

_____

7. Your most important consideration is to
narrow your choices down to the professions
you are most passionate about—not what
others tell you what profession would be
best or most lucrative for you. What is the
profession that will leave you motivated and
looking forward to every day? Remember,
you want to select a profession that will
give you joy and satisfaction for the
next thirty to forty years of your life.

_____

_____

_____

_____

_____

8. Find people who are already in the professions
you are considering like wildlife biologists,

wildlife managers, university faculty and ask them about their careers. Who do they work for? They may work for county, state, federal natural resource agencies, universities or private conservation organizations. What is their sense of accomplishment for the work they have done? What trends do they see for the future for opportunities in their profession relating to desired skills, abilities, and advances in technology?

_____

_____

_____

_____

_____

9. Visit the schools you are considering and talk to graduates from those schools in to obtain an opinion of their experiences and satisfaction with their education at that school. If possible, connect with faculty members of the disciplines you are most interested in pursuing to get an impression of how well you relate to them.

_____

_____

_____

_____

_____

Dr. Eugene P. Odum, photo courtesy of the University of Georgia, Marketing and Communications. He was the mentor who motivated me to design my graduate education around ecology-based conservation.

Lesson 2

Choosing a grad school. If you want to be the best, learn from the best: "Learn from the one who wrote the book!"

When considering my graduate school options, *if I wanted to be the best, I should study under the best*. My main interest was in pursuing ecology related to wildlife conservation. Dr. Eugene P. Odum was the University of Georgia (UGA) professor who wrote the highly acclaimed college textbook *Fundamentals of Ecology*, and he created the Institute of Ecology at UGA. He was subsequently a recipient of the Crafoord Prize in 1987, the biologist's equivalent of the Nobel Prize.

There was another consideration that played into my decision on where to attend graduate school. I grew up in central Iowa and rarely traveled more than twenty-five miles from home. I got two invitations for graduate study at the University of Wisconsin and at the University of Georgia. I desired to benefit from learning ecology from Dr. Odum, but I also felt it would be beneficial to go to UGA to expand my horizons beyond the Midwest. It was the right decision! In graduate school at the UGA I focused on my *trilogy of interests* which included ecology, wildlife management and communications. I graduated with a four point grade record because I studied what I loved!

There is an extra dimension to selecting a graduate school. First, select a graduate school that excels in your desired field of study. In my case, I was looking at schools that had a reputation for their accomplishments in the evolving discipline of ecology.

Seek out the person or persons who have played a pivotal role in your field of choice. Follow up by contacting them to explore the options for attending their university to study under them. In my case, it was Dr. Eugene P. Odum, often considered the *founding father of ecology*. He was the *idea man* and inspiration on the cutting edge of the ecology movement in the 1970s. I wanted to learn from *the one who wrote the book*! My efforts succeeded. He personally invited me to attend UGA, and I eagerly accepted the opportunity.

Workbook questions and notes

1. What are the graduate schools that have the most appeal to you for the career you wish to pursue?

_____

_____

_____

_____

_____

2. Are there any faculty members in those graduate schools who have excelled in their career field and demonstrated national leadership and vision in that discipline including books or publications?

_____

_____

_____

_____

_____

3. How can you contact faculty members to inquire about opportunities for study under that person at that school.

_____

_____

_____

_____

_____

4. Visit your schools of interest to get a feel for the learning environment and faculty at the schools.

_____

_____

_____

_____

_____

Carrol Henderson realized that media skills are an important skill for promoting wildlife conservation. Here he is sharing news about the DNR Nongame Wildlife Program on Minnesota Public Radio

Lesson 3
Cross-pollinate your grad school major.

My graduate studies initially included ecology, forestry and wildlife management. Then I crossed over to the liberal arts campus at UGA and took courses in journalism, feature writing and public relations. I also took a class under Dr. Archie Patterson in the School of Forest Resources in *informational methods* to enhance my skills for appearing on radio and TV to promote wildlife conservation. This hybrid mixture of skills and education gave me a competitive edge in a world where most job applicants are specialized only in a single major or skill set.

Workbook questions and notes

1. After narrowing down your choice or choices for a graduate school, inquire about the opportunities that exist at that school for coursework in the fields or disciplines that would complement your major.

   _____

   _____

   _____

   _____

   _____

2. Examine the coursework you are planning and see what classes could be added in your curricula in either undergraduate or graduate coursework. Consider what supplemental coursework could enhance your appeal to potential employers.

   _____

   _____

   _____

   _____

   _____

3. What are the supplemental topics or classes
that you feel would best add to your skillsets
in your chosen profession? e.g. writing,
speaking, media skills, a foreign language
or data management skills.

_____

_____

_____

_____

_____

Photography skills are also important for promoting wildlife conservation.

Lesson 4
Develop personal skill sets that will enhance your career.

Don't underestimate the importance that personal skill sets can add to your appeal when applying for work. I learned skills for photography, popular writing, public speaking, and international travel which became invaluable for my effectiveness in leading Minnesota's Nongame Wildlife Program. I was able to use many of my photos in the five DNR books I wrote, and I presented hundreds of slide shows and PowerPoint presentations over the course of my 44-year career in the DNR. My knowledge of Spanish and travel experience in Costa Rica also helped immensely with promoting international conservation efforts in Costa Rica.

Photography skills

After I casually mentioned that I would like to try 35 mm. photography while home on leave from the Air Force, my father bought me a used Argus Rangefinder 35 mm. camera as a birthday gift in 1972. I received it while I was stationed at Keesler Air Force Base in Biloxi, Mississippi. I won several awards at the Air Force base photo contest after photographing monarch butterflies in migration that fall in the Biloxi area. Many cameras later, I have won seven awards in national photography competitions and have used hundreds of my photos to illustrate my wildlife books, magazine articles, newspaper stories and PowerPoint presentations about wildlife conservation.

Two photos I took of humpback whales offshore from the Pacific coast of Costa Rica in January of 1990 documented that region as a humpback whale migratory destination and calving area. Those two photos convinced Costa Rican president Oscar Arias to designate over twenty square miles of the Pacific Ocean as the Ballena Marine National Park to protect the whales. Those are the two most important photos I have every taken. Good photos can convey powerful conservation messages. Sharpen your photography skills. Use good equipment. Learn from other skilled photographers, take classes to learn photography techniques, learn to give impactful presentations, and create inspiring conservation messages with your images.

Writing skills

I began writing articles at the Department of Natural Resources for their Minnesota Volunteer magazine in 1976. Since then, I have written thirty-nine articles for the Volunteer, fifteen books, many magazine and newspaper articles, and hundreds of news releases about nongame wildlife conservation projects.

Writing is an essential skill for developing support and understanding for your program and for sharing your passion. *Keep writing!* It gets easier the more you write. Learn to ruthlessly edit your work. Find friends who are good at editing who can help you sharpen your writing skills. Avoid redundancy and meaningless words.

If you wish to write a book, identify a unique perspective that has not been covered by other authors and a topic that will enrich the lives of your readers. For example, I realized there was a significant lack of Minnesota-based information for citizens who wanted to help pollinators or songbirds through landscaping or gardening. Most landscaping books were written for national audiences and included information about wildlife and plant species not in Minnesota. Minnesota conservationists needed *Hands-On* books with techniques and plans to enhance their private land specifically written for Minnesotans as well as information on building nest boxes and bird feeding techniques.

Public speaking skills

Learn to present in front of people in a clear, pleasant and entertaining manner. *Some people are more afraid of public speaking than they are of death!* There are unfortunately some natural resource experts who are introverts who avoid reporters, public forums, presentations and media contacts. This is sadly a missed opportunity to generate support for the wildlife conservation and natural resources that we care about! Supervisors and program managers need to look for those presentation skills in the people they are hiring. Avoid the introverts.

International travels

Take advantage of international travel and study opportunities when you are young, single and not limited by family and parenting obligations. Charles Darwin wrote: "…there can be nothing more profitable for a young naturalist than a journey to distant countries."

While in grad school, my wildlife professor, Dr. Jim Jenkins, stopped me in the hall one day and asked me "How would you like to go study in Costa Rica?" I said "Sure!" and then I went to look up where it was. It was a life-changing experience. Dr. Jenkins was an innovative and inspirational mentor during my graduate years. He was the co-inventor of the hypodermic dart gun for capturing wildlife, and he spent a year as a visiting professor teaching at the University of Praetoria in South Africa.

I applied for and was accepted for a two-month course in tropical agriculture and land use through the Organization for Tropical Studies (OTS) at the University of Costa Rica in February and March of 1969. I was also accepted for a second course in principles of tropical ecology in July and August of that year. I drove to Costa Rica with Dr. Jenkins in an old $250 pickup for the second OTS course. It was the beginning of a marvelous life-changing experience where I met my wife Ethelle Gonzalez Alvarez at the freshmen orientation dance at the University of Costa Rica in 1969. We have now been married for fifty-five years. My OTS coursework dramatically broadened and intensified my international perspective on ecology and wildlife conservation.

In 1985 Ethelle and I were visiting her family in Costa Rica when we ran into our travel agent, Karen Johnson. She was escorting Minnesota Vikings football coach Bud Grant and some of his friends on a fishing trip. We shared a happy hour visit with Karen, Bud and his friends at El Bramadero restaurant in Liberia. We had a wonderful time visiting with Bud and learning about his interests in wood ducks, a pair of ravens he had raised as a kid, and other wildlife. He never mentioned football. Later I arranged to meet Bud at the Vikings practice facility in Winter Park with DNR cinematographer Larry Duke. There we produced television public service announcements from Bud to promote the Nongame Wildlife Checkoff. Bud also arranged for my friend and bluebird enthusiast John Thompson to place and manage bluebird nest boxes throughout the Viking's Winter Park training facility.

After returning to Minnesota, Karen called and asked if we would be interested in leading birdwatching tours to Costa Rica. We cautiously agreed, not knowing quite what we were getting in to. We led our first birdwatching trip to Costa Rica in 1987. As of 2024, we have led international birding trips throughout Latin America from Guatemala and Cuba to Patagonia, New Zealand, Iceland, Kenya and Tanzania and thirty-two birding trips to Costa Rica.

I have written four field guides for the wildlife of Costa Rica with the University of Texas Press including the 539 page "Field Guide to the Wildlife of Costa Rica." It was published in 2002 using my field notes and photos from leading sixteen trips to Costa Rica since 1987. The field guide covered birds, mammals, reptiles, amphibians, and invertebrates.

The response to this book was amazing. It sold over 18,000 copies. In October of 2002 Costa Rican ambassador to the United States, Jaime Darenblum, held a reception and book-signing honoring me at the Costa Rican embassy in Washington, D.C. I was recognized for writing my field guide for Costa Rican wildlife and promoting Costa Rica as a wonderful nature tourism destination that showcases their efforts to preserve their biological diversity. The former Costa Rican president, the minister of the environment, and the Costa Rican ambassador were all in attendance at the reception in addition to representatives from the Smithsonian Institution, National Geographic Society, and the World Bank. I also signed a copy of my field guide for Costa Rican president Abel Pacheco.

The comment by Charles Darwin could not have been more profound: "...there can be nothing more profitable for a young naturalist than a journey to distant countries." Our chance meeting with Karen Johnson and Bud Grant created the opportunity to meet exceptional people, biologists and guides throughout Latin America. We experienced stunning scenery, tropical rainforests and remarkable wildlife from resplendent quetzals to Andean condors, harpy eagles, jaguars and southern right whales!

In 1990 Ethelle and I were leading a birding trip to Peru and visited the famous Inca ruins at Machu Picchu. Our guide was a young woman of Inca descent who shared her insight about the Inca culture. She said their culture had been built upon a lifestyle that embodied three words: *Love, Teach, Learn.* What a memorable lesson for leading a meaningful life!

Mentorship presentation responses

Your talk to my Honors Mentor Connection was inspirational. Your passion for photography really resonated with me, especially when you showed us your first camera. It was awesome to see that it was a symbol of how it has been such a constant in your life. The story you told us about how two pictures that you took changed the mind of the government in Costa Rica was fascinating.

I am glad that you emphasized the importance of writing and public speaking. Often times, I feel that people tend to believe that writing and public speaking are not related to math and science. However, your presentation has made me realize that writing and public speaking still play an essential role in math and science fields because writing and public speaking are needed to effectively communicate results, ideas and theories.

I really admire Mr. Henderson because of his wide range of abilities and talents. On top of being a conservationist, he is a photographer, an author, a tour leader for birdwatching, and a speaker. All those skills are very different but all essential to the job he does. These skills help Mr. Henderson perform his job to the best of his ability. Also, Mr. Henderson was an integral part in restoring bluebirds, bald eagles and trumpeter swans. For that alone, Mr. Henderson is a truly great member of society.

Workbook questions and notes

1. What are some skillsets that you may wish to enhance your appeal to a potential employer? How can you acquire those skillsets?

_____

_____

_____

_____

_____

2. Realize that you can develop proficiency in some of these skillsets on your own-beyond the classroom.

_____

_____

_____

_____

_____

3. Look for events, organizations or publications that can help you improve your skillsets. E.g. Minnesota Nature Photography Club.

_____

_____

_____

_____

_____

Dr. Walter Breckenridge, bluebird and wood duck enthusiast and professor emeritus from the University of Minnesota.

Lesson 5
Find the mentors in your midst who will share their vision, perspective and lifelong passion for nature.

Mentors don't just happen. They grow on you. You eventually realize they have qualities for the kind of person you want to become. I have been fortunate to have encountered several memorable mentors during my life. They have inspired me with their personalities, their commitment and dedication to wildlife conservation and their sincere friendships.

Roger Holmes, Tom Isley, Dave Vesall and Joe Alexander at the DNR inspired me with their passion for helping wildlife, preserving habitat and their legislative savvy for achieving success with the legislature. Roger taught me to be a good listener, and he was good at editing my technical reports for the Section of Wildlife. We enjoyed many memorable duck, goose and sharp-tailed grouse hunts from the Lac qui Parle Wildlife Management Area in Minnesota to the wetlands of Saskatchewan. One of Roger's most memorable phrases when deciding on a conservation action was an emphatic "It's the right thing to do!"

Dr. Walter Breckenridge taught me that you can be a concerned and involved conservationist until you are a hundred years old. Art Hawkins shared his passion for waterfowl management, keeping good records of his observations, and wood duck conservation. Art had the ultimate mentor. Art was a graduate student of Aldo Leopold in the 1930s. He passed on Aldo's passion for wildlife conservation throughout his life.

Dr. Bud Tordoff's passion for peregrines was infectious. His passion for making the restoration of peregrines a success was obvious through his extensive networking contacts with falconers. At Bud Tordoff's memorial service, a former graduate student said one thing he remembered about Bud is that every morning he would gather up his graduate students and have a coffee break with them. That is where they really got to know each other and become inspired by Bud. They discussed their research projects as well as their latest woodcock hunting forays. I knew some people at the DNR who would never go for a coffee break. They never got to know other DNR staff members or appreciate the value of connections made over those informal coffee breaks.

Dr. Pat Redig similarly inspired me with his broad knowledge of raptors and ability to plan and execute research not only on peregrines but also on research linking lead poisoning in bald eagles to the use of lead ammunition for both waterfowl hunting and deer hunting.

Dr. Dan Janzen, one of my mentors in the Organization for Tropical Studies and an inspiration for preserving biodiversity in the tropical dry forests in Latin America.

Dr. Daniel H. Janzen, a tropical entomologist from the University of Pennsylvania, inspired me with his dedication, hard work, enthusiasm, ability to keep up with the latest scientific technology and his determination to preserve tropical dry forests in Costa Rica. He discovered many new insect species and even named one of them after our son Craig. He received the international Crafoord Prize in 1984 for his professional accomplishments. That is the biologist's equivalent of the Nobel Prize.

These mentors provided me with a gold standard throughout my career for building professional and personal friendships, continuing personal development, learning the value of networking, demonstrating their lifelong dedication to wildlife conservation and respectful treatment and supervision of their employees and conservation partners. I would like to think that some of their passion, knowledge and dedication was passed on to me in my wildlife conservation career, and I hope I have passed some of that passion on to my own friends and colleagues.

Mentors may emerge for you as they share their wisdom and experience with you. Their influence is a gift that will inspire you throughout your life. Mentorship begins as friendship and matures into a bond of understanding and inspiration for lifetime themes you both care about. May there be special mentors in your future to guide your career.

Workbook questions and notes

1. What are the qualities in a mentor that will be of particular value to you?

_____

_____

_____

_____

_____

2. Are there already mentors in your life who have already inspired you?

_____

_____

_____

_____

_____

3. Realize that you may become a mentor for someone who admires your skills and accomplishments. Help them develop their own professional skills.

_____

_____

_____

_____

_____

Carrol Henderson holds an immature common loon ready for banding as part of the research on the effects of the Deepwater Horizon oil spill on Minnesota bird life.

The author enjoying his "dream job" as a wildlife manager with a newly banded Canada goose at the Lac qui Parle Wildlife Refuge in 1975.

Lesson 6

In picking your job, don't follow the dollars. Follow your heart.

After completing my graduate education at the University of Georgia in 1970 and my Air Force service in 1973, I was hired by DeLeuw, Cather and Company in Atlanta, Georgia, to be an ecological consultant to plan a four-lane tollway corridor from Chattanooga, Tennessee to Tallahassee, Florida. My salary was $15,000 per year. Upon completing the six-month project, I was to be transferred to their home office in Chicago. I was then offered a job by the Minnesota Department of Natural Resources as assistant manager of the Lac qui Parle Wildlife Refuge at a salary of $10,000/year. *I accepted the job in a heartbeat!* DeLeuw, Cather offered to match that salary, but I said that was not the point. Becoming a wildlife manager was the dream job I had always wanted.

Don't be deceived by the amount of your paycheck. If you hope to experience sustained success in your career, you need to find a profession that you will find personally fulfilling every day of your career. The size of your paycheck will be a secondary consideration. Now, fifty years later, I am convinced it was the right decision.

Mentorship presentation responses

You truly changed my perception of having a successful life. A successful life is not about physical wealth. It's about doing what you love.

Often, I feel people go into certain professions and careers because it is what their parents think they should do or what makes a lot of money. I really want to find a career that I go to work every day and enjoy every day, so I think it is wonderful that you brought attention to that.

I really enjoyed today's seminar because I felt it was focused on chasing dreams. I always feel like I am pressured to pick a career that has a high salary like a doctor or a lawyer. However, I have so many other ambitions that my parents don't really support because I would end up not making a lot of money. I enjoyed how today's presenter has disproved all those speculations and doubts and is truly happy with his job. He has obtained success in something he truly has passion about. That is what makes life fulfilling.

Workbook questions and notes

1. Think about the kind of work you want to do as you enter the prime of your life. Consider where you want to live to enjoy your preferred lifestyle, and of course consider how you will live within your budget. In my case, I also found that accepting a job with the State of Minnesota Department of Natural Resources provided a good working environment, job security, health coverage and long-term retirement

benefits. Those benefits supplemented the salary that I may have felt was limited at the time.

_____

_____

_____

_____

_____

2. There are many other positions available in natural resource/ wildlife conservation positions in public and private agencies. They include county governments like Three-River Parks and Dakota County and county governments with forestry offices; state agencies like the Board of Soil and Water Resources, Pollution Control Agency, Minnesota Zoo, DNR: Section of Fisheries, Section of Wildlife, Division of Parks and Recreation, Division of Ecological and Water Resources, Division of Enforcement, Nongame Wildlife Program, Minnesota Biological Survey; federal agencies like National Park Service, U.S. Fish and Wildlife Service including local wetland offices and National Wildlife Refuges.

_____

_____

_____

_____

_____

3. There are also some very important positions within conservation organizations like Pheasants Forever and Ducks Unlimited worth pursuing. They are about much more than pheasants and ducks. In recent years they have broadened their focus on creating significant habitat benefits for creatures ranging from butterflies to bluebills. They also create habitat benefits for pollinators and prairie songbirds. They routinely request and receive millions of dollars annually conservation of habitat through the Lessard-Sams Outdoor Heritage Council which allocates the funding from a 3/8 of 1 percent sales tax on retail sales in Minnesota. There are also graduate research opportunities at universities like the University of Minnesota, Brainerd Community College, Bemidji State University, Crookston and the Natural Resources Research Institute in Duluth.

_____

_____

_____

_____

_____

4. It is important to do your homework among these various employers. Identify the kind of work opportunities they offer. Identify the kind of work you wish to tackle as you begin your career.

_____

_____

_____

_____

_____

Lesson 7
Learn to *Connect the Dots!* Learn to connect two apparently unrelated facts or ideas to solve a problem.

Connecting the dots is a unique skillset that increases your potential to recognize opportunities for success through creative initiatives. This involves connecting two apparently unrelated topics and linking them to create a unique revelation for understanding or resolving a problem. After taking on my new position as the DNR Nongame Wildlife Program supervisor in 1977, I read an article about a study in the Journal of American Veterinary Medical Association about a bald eagle that had died after consuming about seventy-five lead shotgun pellets at a national wildlife refuge in Maryland. The pellets had been ingested because the eagle had been feeding on dead geese that had been shot and not retrieved by hunters at the refuge. This was the first article I had seen about a connection between waterfowl hunting with lead shotgun pellets and lead poisoning causing the death of federally listed bald eagles.

Bald eagles learned to prey on Canada Geese at the Lac qui Parle Wildlife Refuge. Photo courtesy of Steve Hennis, MDNR

Those were the same conditions that existed at the Lac qui Parle Wildlife Refuge where I had worked for three years! I recalled the dying bald eagle I had picked up at the refuge in November of 1974. It had symptoms of lead poisoning that I had not recognized at the time. Three years later, I initiated a research project to verify if Lac qui Parle's eagles were being poisoned by exposure to the lead shotgun pellets. The research verified they were being poisoned by lead ammunition used for goose hunting. This resulted in the use of lead ammo being banned for waterfowl hunting in Minnesota in 1991, and in 1997 it was banned for waterfowl hunting nationwide.

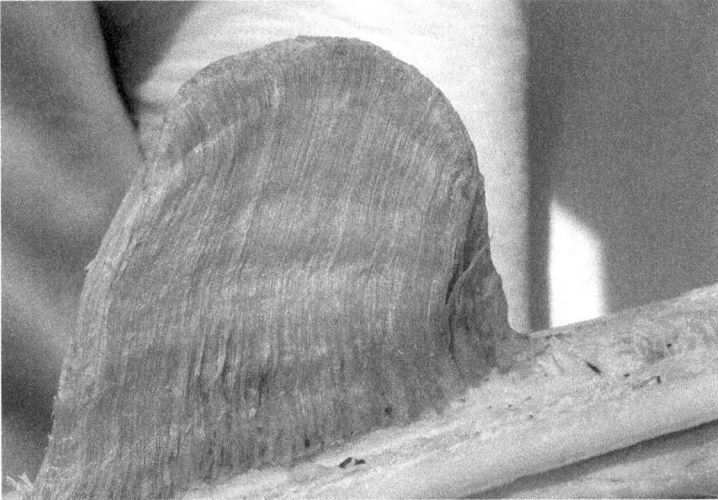

White pelican bill knobs grow each winter on their wintering grounds in the Gulf of Mexico. I believed they would reflect the presence of petroleum contaminants when they were shed in their Minnesota breeding colonies and examined for BP contaminants.

A second example of connecting the dots occurred when I was developing a strategy for research on American white pelicans to determine whether they were adversely affected by the Deepwater Horizon oil spill. We needed to assess the extent of contamination in pelicans nesting at the Marsh Lake pelican nesting colony. We would be capturing nesting pelicans at the colony to obtain blood samples and unhatched pelican eggs for petroleum-related contaminants. I wanted another type of validation to tie contaminants in the pelicans to contaminants picked up in the Gulf of Mexico during the previous winter. I knew from my visits to pelican colonies for banding pelicans at Minnesota Lake and Lac qui Parle that the pelicans possessed bill knobs that they grew on their wintering areas in the Gulf of Mexico. Both males and females grew bill knobs each year. Once nesting was completed, they usually shed the bill knobs in the nesting colony. I knew bill knobs grown in the Gulf of Mexico on their wintering grounds should reflect contaminants from the oil spill. We picked up shed bill knobs in the Marsh Lake colony and had them analyzed for BP-related petroleum contaminants by the staff at the University of Connecticut. My hunch worked. BP-related petroleum contaminants were found in the bill knobs. Bill knobs had never been used previously for determination of environmental contamination.

My third example of connecting the dots occurred as I was developing a research strategy for assessing the impact of the Deepwater Horizon oil spill on Minnesota's loons which would have still been wintering in the Gulf of Mexico when the spill occurred in April of 2010. I heard a news story on the radio about a researcher with the US Geological Survey doing a study on loons in Wisconsin and Michigan with satellite transmitters to determine their migration patterns. That sounded like the kind of information we needed for studying the potential impact of the oil spill on Minnesota's loons! I found out the name of the loon researcher, Kevin Kenow, and I called him to learn if he might be interested in doing a comparable loon study in Minnesota. Kevin said that he could make his research team available for an in-depth multi-year research study on the impact of the Deepwater Horizon oil spill on Minnesota's loons. I reassured him that I could write a workplan for the loon study and raise the funding necessary for the research through the Environment and Natural Resources Trust Fund that was derived from the Minnesota lottery.

It all worked out to generate a study from 2011 through 2017 that received $641,000 in funding from the Environment and Natural Resources Trust Fund which is derived from state lottery proceeds. The information generated by the study resulted in $7.7 million being allocated to the Minnesota DNR and the Minnesota Pollution Control Agency for funding made available from Natural Resource Damage and Remediation (NRDAR) funds derived from BP for fines from the damage caused by the oil spill. All this resulted from listening to a radio broadcast and making a phone call.

One additional example of connecting the dots occurred when I was planning for transfer of forty trumpeter swans from the Twin Cities to the Detroit Lakes area for release in the Tamarac National Wildlife Refuge area. Transferring them by trucks would likely expose the swans too much jarring effect on their legs and could lead to lasting injuries.

C-130 Air Force cargo plane being loaded with 40 trumpeter swans for release in northwest Minnesota.

I needed to find a method that would provide a more stable means of transportation for the swans— like a plane. We needed not just a plane. *We needed a bigger plane!* I had served as a captain in the Military Airlift Command in the Air Force from 1970 through

1973. I was in the 4th Mobile Communications Group and had also served as a loadmaster for the C-130 on deployment. A C-130 military transport plane would be the perfect plane for the mission. I had no current connections with the Air Force, but I still recalled how to work within the Air Force structure. I called the Air National Guard unit in Minneapolis. I explained my background experience with the Air Force and asked if they might be willing to arrange a *training flight* with forty trumpeter swans to Fargo, North Dakota. They responded that they would get back to me. They called back a couple days later and said, "It's a go!"

Mission accomplished.

The ability to connect the dots is a unique quality the evolves from learning to connect apparent relationships that can utilized to resolve a problem. There are no simple "rules" to apply this quality. It benefits from voracious reading of current events, reading technological publications and collaboration with coworkers to resolve unique challenges.

Minnesota Birders at the Detroit Lakes birding festival

Lesson 8
Know your publics.

There is no general public. There are unique key publics and conservation partners associated with different wildlife species and habitats. Identify potential conservation partners and network with them. Effective networking is a key to project success. Include people of diverse cultural and ethnic backgrounds among your partners and include youths whenever possible.

Howard Hill was a world-famous archer in the 1930s who shot a longbow that had a draw weight of 110 pounds. He won 196 consecutive field archery tournaments. He was an accomplished bow hunter and pursued game from birds to elephants. One of his most memorable comments about bowhunting came when he said, "When you go hunting afield, you must know absolutely everything about your quarry: what it eats, where it lives, where it sleeps and its daily movement patterns." He continued, "If you don't know all these things when you go afield, you are not hunting. You are just walking in the woods."

The same principle applies to knowing your publics for media promotion. If you do not know who they are, how to communicate with them, and how to motivate them to help achieve your program goals, you are "just walking in the woods."

Every restoration project I have been involved with required a different mix of publics for support, planning, funding and implementation and including the movers and shakers who know how to make things happen. Success will come from working with those publics who are dedicated to helping the species or habitats you are trying to benefit. And be sure to provide sincere and enthusiastic credits to those partners as you share in those successes.

Mentorship presentation responses

Mr. Henderson's most striking advice was about taking advantage of opportunities. I think Mr. Henderson must have a brave character because he would try many opportunities that were out of his comfort zone, such as attending graduate school in Georgia despite never moving out of Iowa. His strong emphasis on networking, which also contributed to his success, is another suggestion I took away from today's seminar.

Workbook questions and notes

1. Consider groups like the state ornithologists' union, herpetological society or other interest groups affiliated with state universities and museums. Other publics include managers and staff at wild bird stores, bird food manufacturers, state park and environmental education center naturalists, county and state wildlife biologists and wildlife managers, staff and naturalists at national wildlife refuges. Other publics include members of the media who like to report stories about wildlife rescues, migration, phenology, nesting season, bird feeding techniques and seasonal locations for wildlife viewing.

2. Knowing your publics is an extremely important component for a conservation career. It builds a support base for your conservation program. Make a list of those publics including their contact information. Keep in touch with them. They can often provide you with timely information about wildlife and special events that can be of assistance with your work.

_____

_____

_____

_____

_____

Carrol and Ethelle Henderson have been married fifty-five years after meeting at the University of Costa Rica in 1969.

Lesson 9
Keep a healthy balance between your professional and personal life

Sometimes we become so obsessed with our work that we throw too much effort into our professional life and our home and family life suffers. Some program managers or supervisors are controlling micromanagers who think that they must do everything themselves. They will not delegate authority to accomplish their mission. They end up putting in sixty to eighty hours or more per week to get the job done. That pace cannot last, and that approach is not sustainable. They come in on Friday nights and weekends to work; they feel that they cannot afford to let any aspect of their job go undone and often are unwilling to delegate authority. They also expect people who work for them to put in similar long hours. Don't fall into that trap. They will burn you out.

Family life is # 1

Whenever I hire someone, *I tell them that their personal and family life is Number One and that their job is Number Two in priority.* I tell them that within the scope of everyone's life, a day will come when there will be some major crisis relating to health, an accident or other problem affecting them, their spouse, their children or their parents. They need to drop everything to deal with that problem. I ask them to let me know when that is happening and how we can help. We will cover things at work until their problem can be resolved. This gives people an incredible peace of mind so they can deal with their personal problems until they get their life back under control.

This life lesson is essential for the foundation of a successful career. An important part of that career is avoiding an imbalance in priorities that can cause home and family life to suffer. There are obviously issues and opportunities that arise requiring time away from home on evenings and weekends for dealing with problems or making presentations at meetings and conferences. However, that time needs to be balanced to maintain a forty-hour work week.

Avoid the temptation to stay longer hours at work or to go in to work on evenings and weekends. Take the time to enjoy your personal and family life and your personal hobbies.

If you wish to make a difference, work smarter, not longer. Schedule your time and priorities to make your forty hours per week meaningful. Channel your efforts to positive outcomes. Try to avoid office distractions. However, take time out for coffee breaks to have informal time to get to know your peers and job partners. In this current world of working remotely, those coffee breaks have become obsolete. They can be scheduled with your staff at offsite coffee shops.

Mentorship presentation responses

> Your talk helped to re-spark my interest in bird watching with my father as it helped me to redefine the important role played by birds in Minnesota's ecosystems.

> Carrol Henderson showed his passion with his family. When speaking of his son, he just glowed with love along with his proudness. When speaking of his

wife I was as if it was the only type of love that occurs in a story book. Hearing about what he did with the trumpeter swan was so inspiring and hearing his close and personal stories with animals just makes me want to go out and work harder to preserving some of our natural life...

I hear people say, "work smarter, not harder" so much that it is essentially a platitude, but when I heard you say, "work smarter, not longer," the saying caught my attention like the glimmer of a diamond that was almost overshadowed by the cliché treasures of gold and silver surrounding it. Working longer can easily lead to burnout and a decrease in efficiency that could be bypassed through working smarter, not longer.

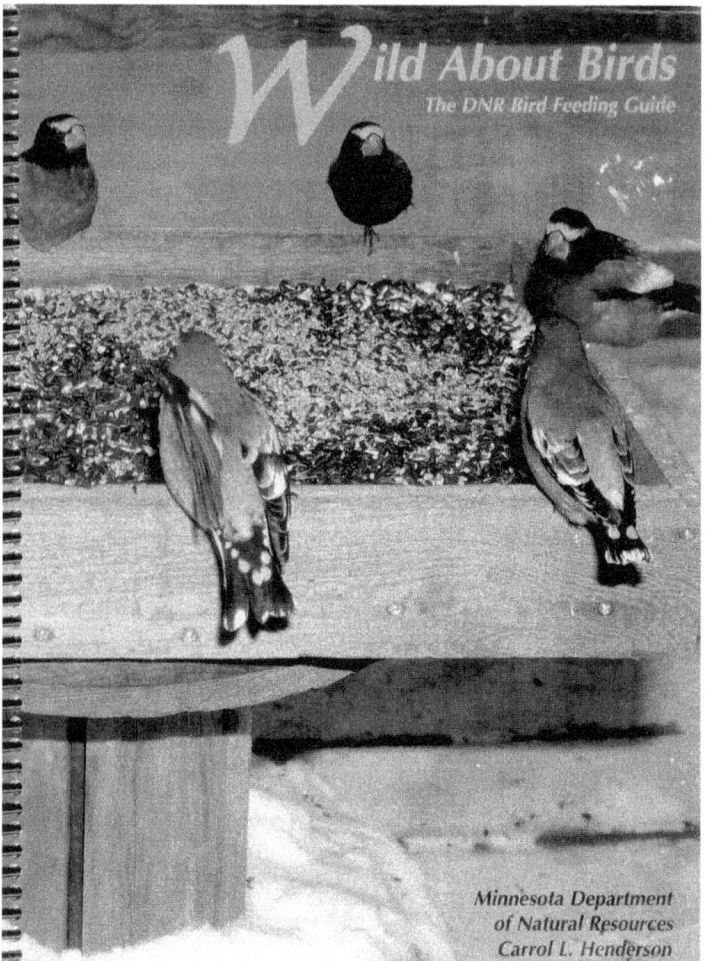

Wild About Birds: the Minnesota Bird Feeding Guide
was written while maintaining a fixed schedule to
maintain a balance with my other job responsibilities.

Lesson 10
Channel your energies, keep the big picture in mind, think big and be patient.

My goal was to manage and restore Minnesota's protected wildlife to healthy and diverse levels. *Channel your energies to fulfill your goals* somewhat like an actor does to channel their personality to become their movie character. Jim Carrey is an example of an actor who "channeled" himself into the many characters he portrayed to give his best performances. Channeling in this case means managing your time, attention and priorities to avoid distractions. When I was writing my book *Wild About Birds: the DNR Bird Feeding Guide*, I would set aside my other work every afternoon at 1:30 and

I worked on the book until I left work for my carpool at 4:00. That way I made steady progress without impairing my progress on other activities.

Keep the big picture in mind, and don't be afraid to think big. What is your long-term vision for your professional goals? Don't let small problems, obsessions with minutia or distractions with social media let you lose sight of your overall goals. Big projects often have the best chance for funding and approval. They may also require years of effort to achieve the desired results. It helps to be patient, thorough, determined, creative and stubborn when necessary.

Mentorship presentation responses

The recovery of Minnesota's swans is one of the most wonderful things I have ever heard about, and to think that Mr. Henderson achieved that in a department which originally only had a budget of $30,000 is a little overwhelming. I thought it was amazing how he almost single-handedly grew the department and finally received sizable federal funding.

Mr. Henderson reminded us to think big and ask the ridiculous questions

because you might just get a yes. Mr.
Henderson also encouraged us to take
advantage of opportunities to study
abroad and learn from experts.

---

1. Channeling is an effort typically associated with a major project involving a larger budget, more staff and a longer time for planning and implementation. It is easy to get carried away with the significance of the project and your determination to make it a success. If you try to impose those priorities onto your existing activities and workload routine, you face an operational train wreck among your priorities. One way to avoid this problem is to specifically allocate a certain me frame designated daily to work on your special project or perhaps one or two days each week to work on the special project when other distractions are off limits.

2. When I was writing *Wild About Birds: the DNR Bird Feeding Guide.* I set aside 1:30 to 4:00 each afternoon to work on the book at the office-not at home. My staff knew that time was off limits for other issues. I had to leave the office at 4:00 daily because I was in a carpool. That helped keep me from staying late at the office. The book was a success, and over 61,000 copies were sold.

_____

_____

_____

_____

_____

I made this pencil drawing of bluebill ducks from my hospital bed while recovering from Guillain Barré syndrome. At the time I was so weak I could only lift a pencil.

Lesson 11

A problem is just an opportunity that needs to be repackaged. *Attitude is everything!*

I had another strategy for success throughout my professional life. When I was diagnosed with Guillain Barré syndrome (also known as French polio) in 1976, I realized that I could be paralyzed for a long time and that there was also a five to ten percent mortality rate. I decided on the first day of that diagnosis that I would get better. At the most severe point in my affliction, my physical therapy consisted of lifting fishing sinkers. I could still lift a pencil, so I wrote articles for the Minnesota Volunteer magazine about the wildlife of Lac qui Parle Wildlife Refuge and drew wildlife sketches. After three months at

North Memorial Medical Center, I learned to walk again using a walker, and I was able to return home. Throughout the entire recovery period I maintained a cheerful outlook, optimism, patience and faith that I would recover. There were no days that I felt depressed or sad.

Attitude is everything! Your three most important assets in time of crisis are a positive attitude, optimism and an ever present smile. We will all face personal medical or emotional crises during our life for ourselves, our parents and our children. We need to be an inspiration to those around us to find hope and optimism in our situation.

My inspiration from "the plucky plover" in Kenya.

I met Kenyan guide John Ngigi when Ethelle and I were leading a wildlife tour in Kenya in 2000. John related the story of leading a family on a wildlife safari in Amboseli National Park in southern Kenya in September of 1999. They were enjoying wildlife in the virtual shadow of Mount Kilimanjaro. John stopped his van when he spotted a blacksmith plover on its nest. As his tourists focused their attention on the nest, he explained the uniqueness of this relative of the American killdeer. With dapper black, gray and white markings, it is easy to identify by sight and sound. The plover gets its distinctive name from its

metallic, clanging call that sounds like a blacksmith
hitting an anvil with a hammer.

Blacksmith plover

Like other members of the plover family,
the blacksmith plover nest consists of a shallow
depression on the ground. The plover lays one to
four speckled eggs that are pointed at one end. As
everyone was watching the female plover, it stood
up. It was incubating two eggs. There was a problem!
The plover had made its nest on a game trail used
by antelopes and even elephants. No sooner had
John realized the plover's dilemma when he spotted
a procession of fifteen elephants approaching the
plover, single file, on the game trail! The procession
was led by the "matriarch" of the herd-a large female.

There was no way to help the plover. As the matriarch approached, the plover stood up, mantled the nest with its wings and began its clanging call. When the elephant was about ten to twelve feet from the nest, the plover flushed from its nest toward the matriarch! It flew right for a spot right between the eyes of the elephant. It pulled up at the last second to strike the elephant with its breast and slapped the elephant with its wings. It pivoted in flight and returned to its nest, mantling its eggs and calling vociferously.

The startled elephant stopped in its tracks and stared at the plover. The other fourteen elephants stopped when the female halted. Then the plucky plover launched another flight at the matriarch, striking it again between the eyes with its breast and slapping it with its wings. The plover peeled off after striking the elephant and returned to its nest, mantling the eggs and calling loudly. A person who understands elephants knows that when an elephant is really upset and likely to charge it flaps its ears. The matriarch began flapping her ears!

It was a classic David and Goliath confrontation. A blacksmith plover weighs about a third of a pound. An adult female African elephant weighs over 6,000 pounds. That is a weight advantage factor of about 18,000 to one! As the matriarch stood flapping her ears, the determined plover launched toward the elephant a third time, again striking it between the eyes and returning to its nest, mantling the eggs and calling loudly.

There must have been some unspoken understanding between these two determined mothers. Each one was defending their family. Slowly, the matriarch stepped off the trail, walked around the plucky plover and returned to the game trail a few feet farther on. All fourteen of the other elephants followed in her footsteps. After they passed, the blacksmith plover stopped calling, settled on her eggs and resumed incubation.

Mentorship presentation responses

Mr. Henderson's happiness was clearly evident when he spoke about his work, and that is what I find truly inspiring. Not only that, but he has been inclined to study wildlife since he was a child, and he is now getting close to seventy years of age, and still going strong. I got the impression that Mr. Henderson is a very ambitious, optimistic and resilient man, considering that he's made such a simply joyous life for himself, so much good has come upon him, even when he was diagnosed with French polio.

Carrol Henderson talked to us about being a wildlife biologist for the Minnesota DNR. He was fascinating. Henderson is clearly an incredibly intellectual man and has lived an exciting life. He has helped major causes and even in just the hour that he spoke to us you can tell that he does everything with passion. One of the main points he got across was just how important your attitude is. His silly psychology story was quite humorous and gave a good message; sometimes the only thing you need to have is an optimistic view. I appreciated his reminder not to try to do everything myself.

Mr. Henderson is a living example of the result of following your utmost passion and giving your all into something that you love, making a career that is both successful and joyful.

This life lesson is all about attitude. If you approach life with a positive attitude, you will not be deterred by the occasional curveball that comes your way. You will look always look forward to the next positive chapter in your life. After returning home from the hospital in October, I took a walk downhill to the pasture below our farmhouse by Lac qui Parle Lake. I had to walk stiff legged because my knees were still weak. Once I reached the bottom of the hill I marveled at the beauty of the lake and the flight of Canada geese flying over the lake.

Then my knees buckled, and I fell to the ground. I discovered I could not stand up from my prone position and there was no one available to help me. I had no walking stick to help me get up. I looked across the pasture and spotted an old wooden fence post about eighty yards away. If I could get to that fence post, I could pull myself up. I crawled on all fours across the pasture and finally reached that old fence post. I pulled myself up to a standing position. I walked stiff-legged back up the hill and finally reached our house. If you encounter a challenging point in life where you feel you are "crawling on all fours," look for someone who can help serve as that proverbial "fence post" who can help you pull yourself up and recover from your difficulties. No matter what challenges you may face, never give up.

Carrol L. Henderson

This loon and its chick represent the very spirit of conservation in Minnesota. They require healthy pristine
lakes, protection from contaminants, diverse natural
shorelines, and hands-on efforts to preserve their
nesting sites.

Lesson 12
Keep a Four-H strategy to balance your conservation program.

I recognized the need for identifying, protecting, and managing four priorities within a comprehensive wildlife conservation program: **Habitats** of primary significance to nongame wildlife. There is also a need for protecting and managing poorly known nongame species considered in a **Holistic** category. They are important ecological components of natural communities. There is a third need to provide benefits to **High-Profile** wildlife species as well-known species that have been neglected and threatened with extirpation or continuing declines. Those species that will generate citizen support and enthusiasm for your initiatives.

Finally, there is a need for getting Minnesota citizens to become personally involved with **Hands-**

On efforts to help wildlife by preserving or restoring habitat, landscaping for wildlife, building and maintaining nest boxes, and doing simple projects like feeding birds. I later realized there was also a **Fifth *H*** needed in my conservation playbook—a ***Historic Perspective***. Citizens need to know how Minnesota's wildlife populations were devastated during the pioneer settlement era and explore our options for restoring those populations.

The author providing a "Get the lead" out presentation for youths who will be participating a DNR State Parks mentored deer hunt.

Lesson 13
Stealth mode

Just do it! There are times that, without breaking any agency rules, you can still make good things happen outside of normal *bureaucracy*. If you don't do it, it won't get done! Following is an example:

Copper Roundtable

There was a Section of Wildlife mandate preventing their employees from discussing the impact of lead ammunition poisoning on wildlife. Without breaking any DNR rules, on August 22, 2012, Lori Naumann and I arranged a gathering of what became the first Copper Roundtable at Davanni's Pizza in Anoka. We were not in the Section of Wildlife. We were in the Division of Ecological and Water Resources, so the Section of Wildlife mandate did not include us.

Attending were Dave Orrick of the St. Paul Pioneer Press, Doug Smith of the Star Tribune, Ryan Bronson of Federal Cartridge, Dr. Pat Redig, Irene Bueno Padillo and Michelle Willette of the U of MN Raptor Center and Alex Gutierrez of the DNR Enforcement Division. Staff from the DNR Section of Wildlife were not allowed to attend. Participants discussed what they knew about this issue and common ground where this topic could be dealt with in an objective and professional manner.

Resulting news stories about the impact of lead ammunition causing lead poisoning bald eagles and the importance of nontoxic ammunition alternatives were subsequently published in the Star Tribune, St. Paul Pioneer Press, Duluth News-Tribune and the Grand Forks Herald. *We helped get the cat out of the bag—exposing the dangers of continued use of lead ammunition on Minnesota's wildlife including federally protected migratory birds.*

Stealth mode is a strategy of last resort, but it can be essential to rising above the bureaucracy when common sense processes are necessary to benefit wildlife. In this case, members of the DNR Section of Wildlife had apparently been prevented from exposing or discussing the toxic dangers to Minnesota wildlife from use of lead ammunition for deer hunting. This mandate was apparently caused by gun rights groups and their lobbyists who influenced the DNR to cover up any negative environmental impacts caused by use of lead ammunition for hunting. There were no DNR rules that said employees outside of the DNR Section of Wildlife could not discuss the issues related to the toxic impacts of lead ammunition on Minnesota wildlife, so we followed Mark Twain's timeless advice: "Always do right. It will gratify some people and astonish the rest."

Local and national television news coverage about trumpeter swan restoration helped immensely to promote the value of wildlife restoration and the Minnesota DNR Nongame Wildlife Program.

Lesson 14
Use the *Multiplier Effect* to spread your conservation messages.

With the same amount of time and effort, you can spread your message to one, ten, one hundred, a thousand or hundreds of thousands of citizens. It is important for people involved in wildlife conservation to sharpen their skills in public speaking and connecting with the media to reach the public with conservation messages. There are still some wildlife biologists in leadership positions who avoid the media. They fail to recruit people who have demonstrated skills to promote wildlife conservation. A failure to connect with the media cripples our programs. We need to hire wildlife supervisors and managers who understand the importance of hiring staff with media competence.

Digital Bridge to Nature teacher workshop on Touch the Sky Prairie

We also need more educational programs to reach youths with compelling messages on wildlife conservation. The *Digital Photography Bridge to Nature* program was an example of implementing the multiplier effect by teaching the teachers-not the students. Over three years, we presented 114 teacher workshops to 1,560 teachers. Each teacher participant provided digital bridge training sessions and photo safari experiences to an average of sixty students. This program is estimated to have reached about 93,600 Minnesota children!

With the same amount of time involved, media connections can also reach thousands of people statewide nationwide and even worldwide. This includes efforts by the DNR Nongame Wildlife Program through the EagleCam and Peregrine Falcon Webcam.

It is also important to realize that you can make reporters look good by giving them great stories. They will come back to you in the future asking what else you are doing that is newsworthy.

Implementing the multiplier effect can greatly improve your effectiveness in reaching your target audience with your desired conservation messages. Doing so involves a thorough knowledge of the many available opportunities for reaching people with your conservation messages.

Mentorship Presentation Responses

Mr. Henderson was an example of how passion can bring one far in life.... It was also very fun to listen to him talk about his previous mentors, and how they inspired him to become what he is today. Also, hls own health condition with French polio show what faith and optimism can really do for a person. Having high dreams, as the worst that can happen is someone says no, is crucial to success and is what will separate the creative from the non-creative.

Workbook questions and notes

List five media outlets that you would use to inform your target publics about a new record of migratory birds like raptors or waterfowl available for viewing in your area.

1. _____

2. _____

3. _____

4. _____

5. _____

Lesson 15

Your success is determined by the extent to which your employees are successful in fulfilling their goals.

Give your employees the *authority, budget* and *flexibility* they need to be both fulfilled and challenged by their work. Then help them achieve their professional goals.

Roger Holmes taught me to *manage my employees by exception.* They were responsible for making routine management decisions, but they were to consult with me when they had questions or issues needing resolution. He taught me not to micromanage employees. *Look for self-starters when you hire new employees! Not introverts.*

Every time you hire a new employee, it is a chance to create a new relationship and long-term partnership for future progress in your program. There are many young applicants in the tech world who change jobs every three to four years as they begin to climb their corporate ladder for success. I discovered the world of wildlife conservation is different for longevity of service. The five regional staff members that I hired at the beginning of the Nongame Wildlife Program in 1981 and 1982 stayed in their original field positions for an average of twenty-four years! Nongame staff members that I subsequently hired stayed with the program from sixteen to thirty-one years.

This long-term dedication is a feature of working in the field of wildlife conservation that is typically overlooked and underappreciated by agency personnel staff. They don't appreciate the significance of job satisfaction that results from the thousands of appreciative citizens who love and support nongame wildlife conservation and the long-term efforts by nongame staff to preserve that wildlife heritage.

The Nongame Wildlife Program includes the opportunity for staff to apply their creative skills and initiatives for wildlife conservation in their particular strong suits. Those abilities may include research, surveys and/or management for the benefit of turtles, bats, purple martins, bluebirds, prairies, boreal forests, bald and golden eagles, peregrine falcons, trumpeter swans, common terns, birding trails, development of educational programs and materials, and media appearances. It also includes creation of lifelong friendships with citizens who care about nongame wildlife. Why would anyone want to leave a job with those meaningful and intangible benefits?

Jan Welsh

Joan Galli

Jan Welsh and Joan Galli are examples of exceptional employees who brought a high level of enthusiasm and dedication to their work in DNR's Nongame Wildlife Program over 30-years of service. Jan was the creative wildlife education specialist who coordinated the statewide Project WILD program and the highly successful Digital Photography Bridge to Nature program. Joan Galli was the enthusiastic and dedicated nongame wildlife program specialist for the metropolitan region, program planner and bat conservation enthusiast. Her interests ranged from bats to frogs, turtles and bald eagles as well as exceptional media advocacy.

Sadly, some supervisors intentionally prevent

employees from experiencing any sense of achievement or success. They are intimidated by employees who are smarter than they are. They require endless meetings to ensure control over their *minions™*, and they obsess over minutia. They require reporting on meaningless details that demoralize and destroy program moral, creativity, initiative and they fail or refuse to acknowledge or reward employees for their achievements. These employees are typically helpless to complain about their treatment, and their only recourse is to file grievances that hopefully will force the rogue supervisors to receive counseling or consequences from higher level personnel officers. It is important for persecuted employees to document their treatment in detail so it will stand up to scrutiny by higher level personnel officers.

Workbook questions and notes

1. What do you believe are the intangible benefits that could be derived from a career in wildlife conservation that would influence you to stay in a position beyond ten years? Give five examples.

   1. _____
   2. _____
   3. _____
   4. _____
   5. _____

2. What are specialty projects or activities that you would pursue in a career of wildlife conservation? Please list five species, habitats or projects of interest.

    1. _____

    2. _____

    3. _____

    4. _____

    5. _____

Helping and attracting bluebirds can become a wonderful "pet project" involving bluebird nest box trails and bluebird photography.

Lesson 16
Always have *a pet project*

Encourage your employees to take on *pet projects* that will be professionally stimulating and rewarding. By that, I mean that you and your professional employees can benefit from a *pet project* within the scope of their position description. There needs to be a tangible product at the end of such a project that makes you feel good about what you do--like publication of a research report, a new initiative (like the DNR Eaglecam,) preservation of habitat, or facilitating a major donation. These projects will sustain inspiration for you over the years. They are a great outlet for your creativity, they generate a positive image for your agency, and they will help you avoid *burnout*.

During my career I found that one of most important factors that sustained my passion for work was to have a succession of *pet projects* in which I was highly motivated and involved over an extended period in addition to my regular work responsibilities and obligations.

Among pet projects that have captivated my passion over the years have been landscaping for wildlife in our backyard, building and managing nest boxes and feeders for birds, writing books like *Woodworking for Wildlife* and *Landscaping for Wildlife*, promoting the Pine-to-Prairie birding trails in Minnesota and Manitoba, developing and implementing the Digital Photography Bridge to Nature program, donations of land to the Nongame Wildlife Program like the Uppgaard Wildlife Management area, and my hands-on involvement with restoration of peregrine falcons and trumpeter swans.

It is important to encourage your employees to select their own pet projects that are within the scope of their job responsibilities. It does wonders for sustaining their long-term dedication, enthusiasm and job satisfaction.

Workbook questions and notes

1.   What are some wildlife conservation pet projects that you might hope to carry out for the benefit of a wildlife species or habitat? Provide five ideas.

1. _____

2. _____

3. _____

4. _____

5. _____

Peregrine falcon feeding its chicks

Lesson 17
Most important wildlife conservation and restoration efforts require not just years, but decades, to accomplish

We live in a world of instant expectations. That does not work with the real world of wildlife conservation. Problems like poaching, illegal killing, habitat loss, wildlife disease issues and pollution cause incremental losses of wildlife over decades. Recovering from those losses may also require decades for restoration.

Legislators may think of their careers in terms of two, four, or six-year terms, with the eventual hope of re-election. Biologists and wildlife managers need infinitely more patience and determination for providing benefits to our environment that sustain and restore wildlife populations and native plant communities. Look beyond your annual work plans to a future perspective on how you are sustaining your long-term goals for "the big picture" in wildlife conservation.

Successful wildlife conservation efforts require long-term commitments from private citizens, organizations, politicians, media and local, state and federal agencies to make those restoration efforts a reality. It requires people to be patient, persistent and stubborn when necessary. An example of recent efforts that have been successful are the restoration of peregrine falcons and trumpeter swans in Minnesota. Current efforts underway include advocacy for hunters and anglers to discontinue using lead ammunition and fishing tackle to stop poisoning our state's loons, trumpeter swans and bald eagles. Nontoxic ammunition and fishing tackle alternatives are increasingly available and economically competitive with lead ammo. Other long term educational and habitat initiatives are necessary to improve habitat management for wood turtles and protection of timber rattlesnakes.

A total of 202 Peregrine Falcons were released in Minnesota through 1989. In 2023, after 35 years of restoration efforts, the population of peregrines had increased to 48 breeding pairs that produced 144 chicks. We began releasing Trumpeter Swans in 1987 and released a total of 374 swans through the mid-1990s. By 2023 the estimate of the state population of Trumpeter Swans was estimated at 50,000 and they were documented to be nesting in 80 of Minnesota's 87 counties. This remarkable increase occurred in 37 years.

Mentorship presentation responses

Mr. Henderson's success shows through the growth of his position and department in the DNR, which started with a few thousand dollars in the '70s and has now been expanded to much more. This amazed me because it represented the substantive impact that Mr. Henderson's ideas were able to have on the perception of the environment and how it can be responded to by those that enable more change, such as the government. His perseverance, success, and overall apparent happiness in life inspired me to stick to what I am passionate about and to make sure I don't sway from the goal regardless of what other more simple opportunities may arise.

Workbook questions and notes

One of the best ways to consider this life lesson is to contact county, state or federal wildlife biologists or wildlife managers to interview them about their careers.

1. Ask them about their long-term involvement with wildlife conservation.

_____

_____

_____

_____

2. How many years have they been at their job?

_____

_____

_____

_____

3. What are the biggest challenges they have faced?

4. What preparation would they recommend regarding technology and special skills?

5. What are their favorite accomplishments and memories?

Books from my library

Lesson 18
Read voraciously. (A room without books is like a body without a soul. -Marcus Tullius Cicero).

Reading is a hobby that begins in childhood and continues through adulthood. Reading can give you a creative and competitive advantage in your work if you keep up with a broad range of books, magazines and conservation organizations. I still have an Iowa songbird foldout poster by Maynard Reece that I kept from the *Picture* magazine in the *Des Moines Register*. It was published on March 12, 1950, when I was just shy of four years old.

My library has grown since the age of five to a collection of over a thousand books. Those books allow me the joy and inspiration of being a "time traveler" who can go back in time more than 160 years with books of exploration from Africa to the Amazon. It allows me to be a world explorer to destinations ranging from the Galapagos Islands to Iceland, Cuba, Patagonia, Africa, New Zealand and Kuwait.

My books allow me to appreciate the art of masters like Luis Agassiz Fuertes, John James Audubon, and John Gould and the natural history, ecological and historic writings of E. O. Wilson, E. Thompson Seton, William Beebe, H. H. Hudson, Eugene P. Odum, Adolph Murie, Alexander Skutch, Aldo Leopold, Rachel Carson, Theodore Roosevelt and even *Birds of the West Indies* by birder James Bond.

My taxonomic books and field guides are not limited just to birds, although I have the complete seventeen volume set of *Handbook of Birds of the World* by Lynx Editions. My other taxonomic guides include *Mammals of the World* by Lynx Editions, *Butterflies of the World*, *Turtles of the World*, *Orchids of the World*, and other wildlife field guides for New Zealand and countries in Africa. These books are invaluable references for my writings, but they are also an inspiration for appreciating the diversity and beauty of our worldwide wildlife.

Whether you create your own collection of books as a nature library or if you do your research and reading online, your reading habits will enhance your accomplishments and keep you up to date on the rapidly evolving technology involved with researching and monitoring our wildlife populations and progress in conservation of our wildlife resources.

Workbook library tips

1. An important component of your library should be a career-based file system of your annual accomplishments and project reports. You might be surprised how often it is necessary to refer to those past reports.

2. It is important to keep involved with professional organizations like The Wildlife Society and conservation organizations like The Nature Conservancy, National Wildlife Federation, Izaak Walton League of America, National Audubon Society, Pheasants Forever and Ducks Unlimited.

3. There are also state level conservation groups the Audubon Society and local division chapters of the Izaak Walton League of America. These organizations will keep you up to date on the latest wildlife conservation developments and legislative initiatives.

4. There are other periodicals that will keep you up to date with conservation initiatives. State conservation agencies like the Minnesota

Department of Natural Resources publish the *Minnesota* Volunteer-a wonderful magazine that comes out six times a year. State level periodicals include publications like *Outdoor News* that keeps you up to date regarding hunting, fishing and other wildlife-related stories including legislative initiatives.

Lesson 19

Some of life's greatest opportunities and revelations come wrapped in a blanket of pure serendipity.

When Dr. Jenkins at UGA asked me "How would you like to go study in Costa Rica?" I said "Sure," and then I went to get a map to find out where Costa Rica was. Grad studies in Costa Rica changed my life, and it was where I met my wife Ethelle!

In 2006, my brother Don told me that he had visited an old farmhouse near Colo, Iowa, where his friend John Handsaker was planning to settle after being married. I followed up to visit the farmhouse of the late farmer and oologist Ralph Handsaker who was John's grandfather. I wrote the book *Oology and Ralph's Talking Eggs* based on the data I gathered from exploring that incredible collection of over 5,000 wild bird eggs from around the world in that old farmhouse.

Sometimes helping wildlife "is a real fluke." An example includes two humpback whale fluke photos I took while leading a birding tour off the Pacific coast Costa Rica on January 29, 1990. Those photos convinced Costa Rican president and Nobel laureate Oscar Arias to create the Ballena Marine National Park to protect the wintering and calving grounds for humpback whales—21.2 square miles!

This photo proved from the pattern on its fluke that it was part of a population of Humpback whales that migrated annually from offshore California to its calving grounds in Punta Uvita region offshore of Costa Rica.

This photo of a Humpback whale also convinced Costa Rican president Oscar Arias to designate over twenty square miles of the Pacific Ocean offshore from Punta Uvita as a national park because it showed a Humpback whale surfacing with the Costa Rican shoreline in the background. These are the two most important photos I ever took.

Mentorship student comments

Mr. Henderson's birding trips began by sheer accident as a result of his international relations. His stories had the underlying theme that if one keeps an open and positive mind, life will present him or her with wonderful opportunities.

Mr. Henderson had what I thought was very useful and important advice about being willing to go boldly trying new things and expanding my skills to promote myself. Mr. Henderson jumped at the opportunity to go to Costa Rica to study ecology there and it ended up changing his life, and he even met his wife. These types of events may happen if I am willing to try new experiences, even if they seem scary, as it may have been for Mr. Henderson who did not even know where Costa Rica was when he first went there.

Author, storyteller, photographer, and above all a leader; these are the priceless words to describe Mr. Carrol Henderson. It was so fascinating to hear of Mr. Henderson's career from his first interview to his high achievements. And the stories about them, they were so full of life and adventure, and fullness. I was and still am still intrigued at Mr. Henderson's words of wisdom, espe-

cially when he talked about working
with people who share your interests.
And that the two assets that shall guide
me are "positive attitude" and an "ever
present smile." What truth!

Carrol Henderson talked about his life
decisions and the importance of wildlife,
and he stuck true to his dreams when he
was growing up. When he was in college,
he switched from engineering to a low
paying industry to stick with his interest,
and he is now a head figure of the DNR.
Henderson started a tiny program that
had a small budget and had the optimism
to keep growing and starting new programs to expand. After success, and more
success, he earned the budget of millions
of dollars and the respect of famous others. His optimism and hard work generat-
ed an imprint on the community and the
preservation of wildlife in Minnesota.

I really enjoyed hearing about your
career path and how your credentials

in not only what you were passionate about helped you with your job, but also the benefits from skills like public relations and public speaking were remarkable. My favorite story was the one you closed with about how the banded swan had come back to you and how that one moment truly represented why you do what you do. It really resonated with me, and your passion for your career is admirable. I hope to love my profession as much as you do.

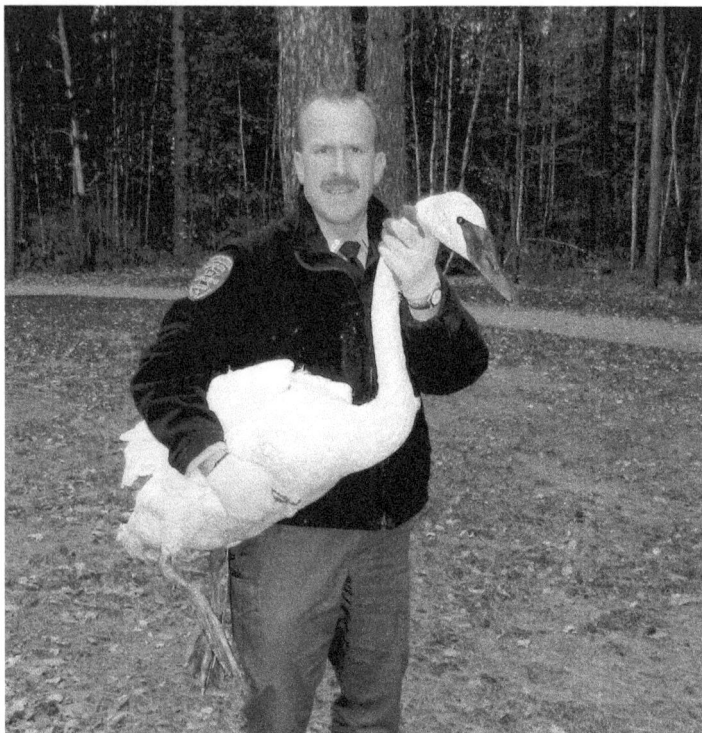

Minnesota Conservation Officer Karl Hadrits with the male Trumpeter swan that stayed with its injured cygnet and allowed itself to be picked up by officer Hadrits so it could stay with it young while it was examined by a vet. Photo by Susan Hadrits.

Lesson 20
Become acquainted with existing laws protecting wildlife and endangered species so you can assist with court proceedings and development of legislation.

Learn techniques for presenting testimony before legislative committees, for testifying objectively against people who have violated game laws and for drafting legislation to improve laws for wildlife conservation. Learn when you need state or federal permits to carry out wildlife conservation projects. Become acquainted with local, state and federal conservation officers. Learn when to contact them regarding enforcement issues, problems or the need for wildlife rescue. Learn presentation skills for testifying before state and federal legislative committees and for providing testimony in court.

An example of the importance of this ability is when "open bait trap sets" were banned by Minnesota law. Until these trap sets were banned, some trappers would surround dead animal carcasses with multiple traps in hopes of catching furbearers like foxes or coyotes. However, those trap sets usually caught low-value furbearers like skunks or opossums, and frequently they caught raptors like Bald Eagles. Some of the eagles were so severely injured that they died. This problem was resolved by a cooperative networking effort among raptor and bald eagle enthusiasts and trappers. The Nongame Wildlife Program teamed up with the staff of The Raptor Center, the DNR Division of Enforcement, and the Minnesota Trappers' Association to draft legislation making it illegal to place traps within twenty-five feet of exposed baits. This significantly reduced the loss of Bald Eagles by accidental trapping.

CLOSING THOUGHTS

"Always do right. It will gratify some
people and astonish the rest."
Mark Twain.

"May we leave many astonished
people in our wake."
Carrol Henderson

About the Author

Wildlife conservationist Carrol Henderson was selected as Minnesota's first DNR Nongame Wildlife Program supervisor in 1977. He continued in that role for forty-one years until his retirement in 2018. His efforts benefited trumpeter swans, peregrine falcons, bluebirds, bald eagles, river otters, ruby-throated hummingbirds, and common terns. His DNR "how-to" books on helping wildlife sold over 300,000 copies. In 2016 he received the national Frances K. Hutchinson award from the Garden Clubs of America as the top conservationist in America. Previous recipients of that award have included Rachel Carson, Walt Disney, Roger Tory Peterson, Ladybird Johnson, and Sigurd Olson.

www.ingramcontent.com/pod-product-compliance
Lightning Source LLC
Chambersburg PA
CBHW030840090426
42737CB00009B/1043